THEN *&* NOW

GLENDALE

OPPOSITE PAGE: Founded in 1892, the Glendale of yesteryear was transformed from a barren desert into a modest town. Homes, stores, buildings, and industries spearheaded the growth and development that lifted Glendale from temperance colony to country town and then into a modern city with fire and police, paved streets, electric lighting, water and sewer systems, libraries, an airport, and a city government. (Image courtesy of Glendale Arizona Historical Society.)

GLENDALE

Debbie Veldhuis

ROAD AVENUES, PUBLIC SQUARES, AND LARGE LOTS
THE   ANTS
S FOREVER FORBIDDEN
IN THE CONVEYANCE OF THE LAND.

School Houses and Churches,
ut no saloons or gambling houses ! No drunken brawls
No jails ! and no paupers !

The design is to furnish opportunities for BEAUTI-
UL, PEACEFUL HOMES, combining as fully
possible the advantages of the city with the security
d quiet and charm of the country. This will be ap-
eciated by a very large class of people. It is the First
olony located in the territory. planned on this basis.

Address:—GLENDALE COLONY CO.,

I am dedicating this book to my mother, Marlene Veldhuis, who instilled in me her love of history, and my sister Diane Veldhuis, who supported all my adventures.

Library of Congress Control Number: 2010920453

Published by Arcadia Publishing
Charleston SC, Chicago IL, Portsmouth NH, San Francisco CA

Printed in the United States of America

For all general information contact Arcadia Publishing at:
Telephone 843-853-2070
Fax 843-853-0044
E-mail sales@arcadiapublishing.com
For customer service and orders:
Toll-Free 1-888-313-2665

Visit us on the Internet at www.arcadiapublishing.com

ON THE FRONT COVER: The Adobe House was the first permanent building constructed at Sahuaro Ranch. Completed in 1887, it was home to Stephen Campbell, the ranch's first manager. Later the Adobe House was used as a residence and office for ranch employees. The Adobe House is said to be the oldest building still standing inside Glendale's city limits. The City of Glendale restored the building to represent its earlier appearance. Today visitors can peek inside for a glimpse how people lived in the past. (Then image courtesy of Glendale Arizona Historical Society.)

ON THE BACK COVER: Over 100 years ago and starting out as a temperance colony, the area that would one day be known as Glendale, Arizona, was settled. In 1920, Grant McArthur offered new and second-hand goods bought, sold, and exchanged. McArthur's was right downtown, located on the corner of Glendale, Fifty-ninth, and Grand Avenues. Now the land is part of the Municipal Office and Parking Complex. Glendale continues to thrive and has become one of the fastest-growing cities in the country. (Image courtesy of Glendale Arizona Historical Society.)

CONTENTS

ACKNOWLEDGMENTS

This book would not have been possible without the support of the Glendale Arizona Historical Society. Their tireless effort to protect Glendale's photographic past is a labor of love for them and underappreciated by the rest of us; so thank you. I especially wish to thank Carol J. Coffelt St. Clair and Charles S. St. Clair. Their book *Glendale* (Arcadia Publishing) was very helpful to me while researching my book.

It would be remiss of me not to also thank others who located and loaned the much needed historical pictures for the book. They are Nelda Crowell (Thunderbird School of Global Management), Mark Swope (John Swope Trust), Sarah Boggan (Thunderbird Medical Center), Maria Hernandez (Arizona Room librarian for the Phoenix Public Library), Lauren Russell (arts-crafts.com), Glendale High School, the Pratt family, the Tolmachoff family, Patricia Zeman (Cabela's), and Louis "Buzz" Sands IV (Sands Chevrolet).

I also need to thank the various colleges and universities as well as Jobing.com Arena and Global Spectrum.

There were also a large number of City of Glendale employees who went out of their way to assist me in locating historical photographs for this book. Especially Ginger S. Eiden (marketing and communications), who supplied names and e-mail contacts for many of my then photographs.

I wish to thank Jared Jackson and Hannah Carney with Arcadia Publishing for their patience in explaining all the nuances of the publishing world and answering my many questions.

Unless otherwise noted, all images are courtesy of the author.

INTRODUCTION

In 1880, the land that is now known as Glendale, Arizona, was nothing more than a vast empty desert. It was home to scorpions and rattlesnakes. This would change, however, when in 1882 William J. Murphy joined three Arizona builders—M. W. Kales, William A. Hancock, and Clark Churchill—to lead the Arizona Canal Company Project. The project was to build 44 miles of canal from the Salt River to the Agua Fria River. This endeavor would bring water to the dry desert land, and where there was water, people and cities would follow.

Murphy and his team completed the canal in May 1885. By the late 1880s, several homesteaders began to settle around the new canal. The first residential area of the city began to rise up out of what was once tumbleweeds and Saguaro cactus.

For Murphy, building the canal turned out to be a financial disaster, so promoting this new land was one way for him to recover from his loses. In 1891, he convinced Burgess A. Hadsell to bring a religious group of 70 families to the area. Glendale was soon on its way to becoming a city, but one different from neighboring Phoenix. While Phoenix had been founded by a bar owner, Hadsell's plan, ironically, was for Glendale to become a religious and temperance colony.

After the turn of the century, more and more families would begin to settle in Glendale. Why the name Glendale was chosen for the new colony in 1885 is not known. With all the effort Murphy put into the developing of the area, many thought it would be named "MurphyVille."

On February 27, 1892 (city's official birthday), the first residential area of the city began to take shape with the Glendale town site taking on its own identity soon after. By the mid-1890s, Glendale had become the pathway for one of the lines of the Santa Fe Railroad. This line linked Glendale to Prescott and northern Arizona. The railroad allowed Glendale settlers to receive building materials as well as transport goods to the north.

Irrigation farming was the area's main occupation as a result of the water resources. This made Glendale an agricultural mecca specializing in lettuce, melons, cotton, and sugar beets. With the development of water and rail service, Glendale now wanted to lure major enterprises to the community. One such growing industry in the United States was sugar beets. Since the early 1880s, a number of sugar beet factories had sprung up in many states for the purpose of turning sugar beets into granulated sugar. Murphy also envisioned a large factory in Glendale for the purpose of producing sugar from the sugar beets grown locally.

By August 11, 1906, a 52,000-square-foot sugar beet factory was built and the Glendale Beet Sugar Factory began operations. Six days later, the first bags of sugar came off the line.

Along with the sugar beet factory was an ice plant for cooling produce shipped by the Santa Fe Railroad. Both sites brought new people to town as well as small business ventures.

The town's first library was founded by Victor E. Messinger. He came to Glendale in 1895, and with him he brought 400 books from his own collection. This collection would be the catalyst for the city's first permanent library built on what is now Murphy Park.

In 1895, there were also 300 residents who called Glendale home, so the first school was built. It was known as Glendale Grammar School and still stands today as Landmark Elementary School. The Glendale State Bank opened its doors in 1909.

World War I brought a new wave of life into Glendale, which officially incorporated as a town in 1910. At this time, the town's population was approximately 1,000.

With cotton reaching $2 a pound and the demand for food high, farmers were kept busy. Soon Glendale needed more housing, and today's Catlin Court was born. Most of these homes, from 1915 to about 1930, are still standing and are on the National Register of Historic Places.

The town's population continued growing and reached 2,727 in 1920. By 1930, the town was now officially the City of Glendale with a population of 3,665. The new city of Glendale would continue to grow. The infusion of WPA money from 1933 also helped to sustain the area, and by 1940 the population had risen to 4,855.

War would once again stimulate growth in Glendale. World War II and both Thunderbird and Luke Fields brought servicemen, their families, and their money to Glendale. Thunderbird Field would later be sold to become the American Institute for Foreign Trade. This new military and college presence ignited the need for additional schools, utilities, and streets.

Development from 1950 to 2000 skyrocketed, resulting in Glendale becoming a major city that was attracting not only new residents, but new businesses. Between 1990 and 2000, Glendale was the 19th fastest-growing city in the nation, with a growth rate of 59.6 percent between 1990 and 2005.

Today the city of Glendale has approximately 236,000 residents and is the fourth-largest city in Arizona. It has rapidly become the West Valley's premier destination for entertainment and shopping. Glendale is also a sports destination with the Jobing.com Arena that is currently home to the National Hockey League Coyotes and state-of-the-art University of Phoenix Stadium (with its retractable roof and roll-out field) that is home to the National Football League Arizona Cardinals. Glendale hosted the 2008 Super Bowl and is home to the Fiesta Bowl. The stadium hosts various expositions, trade shows, motor-sport events, and even a Rolling Stones concert on November 8, 2006. Baseball fans have not been forgotten with Glendale Stadium, which opened in the spring of 2009. The Glendale Camelback Ranch Spring Training Facility is considered a state-of-the-art ballpark, is the league's largest facility, and is the new home for the Chicago White Sox' and Los Angeles Dodgers' spring-training activities.

For the outdoors person, Glendale is now also the site of one of the nation's largest Cabela's sporting-goods stores. In addition to selling boats, fishing, and camping equipment, the store maintains a large aquarium and lifelike animal displays, and it is considered a tourist attraction as well as retailer.

Everything old is new again in Glendale as it embraces its past with Historic Downtown Glendale's Old Towne and Caitlin Court Districts. These quaint shops are restored dawn-of-the-20th-century buildings that offer a variety of antiques, boutique items, as well as dining. There is also the Cerreta Candy Company. This family-owned business was founded 40 years ago and offers daily factory tours. Glendale is also home to "Arizona's Best Family Farm"—the Tolmachoff Farms. This family-run land offers fresh produce, a huge annual maze, seasonal events, and field trips. This fourth-generation farm is owned and operated by one of the city's early Russian families.

Today what was once a temperance colony has progressively changed into a major urban community and one of the fastest-growing cities in the country.

CHAPTER 1

FROM WATER A TOWN GREW

Pictured here is downtown Glendale in the late 1920s looking south along First Avenue (Fifty-eighth Drive) and Glendale Avenue. This was a time when horses had the right-of-way and hitching posts were located along the park. The structure to the right is the Ryder Building that would be part of the city library's history. The city of Glendale celebrated its 100th birthday in 2010. (Courtesy of Glendale Arizona Historical Society.)

There was no Glendale, Arizona, in 1880. The land was nothing more than empty desert and home to rattlesnakes and cactus. But in 1882, William J. Murphy joined three Arizona builders that would bring water to the desert by constructing a canal. From this 44-mile-long canal the town of Glendale grew, and where cactus stood watch, there are now homes and businesses. (Then image courtesy of Glendale Arizona Historical Society.)

FROM WATER A TOWN GREW

Glendale, Arizona, was incorporated on June 18, 1910, but Glendale's history began in 1883, when the Arizona Canal Company hired William J. Murphy to organize the building of a canal from the Salt River to the barren Northeast Valley. The project took nearly two years and when finished brought agriculture and families to the new community. Today what was once predominantly farming has progressively changed into a major urban community and one of the fastest-growing cities in the country. (Then image courtesy of the Phoenix Public Library.)

In the 1940s, travelers knew they were in Glendale by the large neon sign suspended above the intersection of Grand Glendale and Central (now Fifty-ninth) Avenues. The sign was removed in August 1951. Today visitors are greeted at the city's boundaries by Glendale's official logo of three pillars, seen here at Forty-third and Glendale Avenues. The three pillars represent the three strengths of Glendale's community—people, government, and business—all working together. (Then image courtesy of Glendale Arizona Historical Society.)

Glendale was incorporated in 1910 and had a population of approximately 1,000 residents. In 1920, the population rose to 2,727 and then to 4,800 in 1940. During the 1950s, the population nearly doubled to 8,179. With the annexation of nearby Maryville in May 1961, Glendale's population soared to over 30,000. Between 1964 and 1975, the city's population grew from 42,000 to 67,000. As of July 2008, the population for Glendale was reported to be 251,522. (Then image courtesy of Glendale Arizona Historical Society.)

An open irrigation ditch flows past a farm at Olive Avenue and Lateral 16. (Laterals were the roads running north and south along the canals.) Today this lateral is Forty-third Avenue and was once just outside of Glendale. Now it is one of the first boundaries separating Glendale from Phoenix.

Where run-down shacks used in the past by itinerant farm laborers once stood, retail stores and fast-food restaurants now stand. Also gone is the open earthen irrigation ditch. (Then image courtesy of Glendale Arizona Historical Society.)

In 1960, Glendale's then city manager Stan Van de Putte accepts a new 50-star flag. City hall was then in the old Bank of Commerce. It is now in Glendale's municipal office building and garage complex. Completed in 1985 and located at 5850 West Glendale Avenue, city hall was designed by Glendale architect Robert Sexton. Behind city hall, where the amphitheater is, was once a road where, years ago, a singer named Martin David Robinson decided to use the name Marty Robbins. (Then image courtesy of Glendale Arizona Historical Society.)

Glendale was the only city in the state with 100 percent of its streets paved by 1948. Before being paved, the roads lay thick with dust in dry weather and were rutted from wheels. After a rain, they were a muddy mess. The Rainbow Theater, located west of the park, opened in 1911. Today the city's Glendale Municipal Office Complex stands where people once watched talkies. In 1910, Glendale was only 1 square mile in size, but it has now grown to over 56 square miles. (Then image courtesy of Glendale Arizona Historical Society.)

The Phoenix Railway Company provided streetcar service between Phoenix and Glendale from 1911 until 1925, when the line stopped operating because of financial problems. It had five "big yellow" interurban cars that made 10 trips daily. The service was advertised as a "pleasant outing." The tracks were removed in the 1940s, but everything old is new again as the city prepares to have an extension of the Valley Metro Light Rail transit line. (Then image courtesy of Glendale Arizona Historical Society.)

FROM WATER A TOWN GREW

When Dial-A-Ride started in 1975, it was contracted out to Yellow Cab. It consisted of two Dodge vans that served a 3.5-square-mile area, and ridership was 33,000. The city took over operation in 1977 and increased the number to six minibuses. Now Glendale's Dial-A-Ride currently operates a total of 36 minibuses. The area serviced has expanded to over 55 miles, and as of the city's 2009 fiscal year, the ridership was just under 90,000. (Then image courtesy of City of Glendale.)

The 1,000-seat grammar school auditorium served as Glendale's major performing-arts center for several decades. Until the mid-1980s, a community building was used. Then, in 1999, the Glendale Civic Center opened. Situated at 5750 West Glenn Drive, where the old police and court building was located, the $8.5 million facility covers 33,800 square feet and accommodates up to 1,300 guests. Featuring brick and sandstone, and capped with a majestic metal dome, the center is an example of neoclassical architecture. (Then image courtesy of Glendale Arizona Historical Society.)

The Glendale Chamber of Commerce had an office on 5708 West Glendale Avenue until 1969. It shared this location with the optical center, First Federal Savings Bank, and Union Title Company. Today it is home to Southwest Business Machines and Southwest Gas. When the chamber first moved, it was into the city's community building, and there it remained until constructing its own structure in 1987 at 7105 North Fifty-ninth Avenue. Today the chamber serves over 900 area businesses. (Then image courtesy of Glendale Community College.)

FROM WATER A TOWN GREW

The current Glendale City Court is located at 5711 West Glendale Avenue. A new building is under construction at the former Larry Miller Car Dealership site at 4701 West Glendale Avenue. The structure had been abandoned when the auto dealership moved to a new location. The building of the new court complex is part of the city's efforts to revitalize the Glendale Avenue Corridor. The demolition started at the end of June 2008. (Then image courtesy of Mark S. Chapman; now image, City of Glendale.)

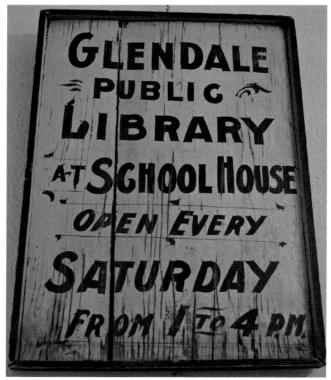

The Glendale Public Library system has grown from meeting in the schoolhouse every Saturday to three locations open seven days a week. The library has a variety of special events, concerts, and lectures both inside its buildings as well as on its grounds. Glendale Public Library system has a main library and two branches, Foothills and Velma Teague. It is the oldest library in the Phoenix metro area, serving residents since 1895. (Then image courtesy of the Glendale Public Library.)

In 1895, Vic Messenger came to Glendale, bringing with him 400 books to donate, and created Glendale's first public library. Two years later, he built a library on the north end of the Ryder Lumber Company to house the collection. Soon others began donating their books. The library moved several times until 1917, when the small pagoda-like roof building was constructed in Murphy Park. The structure became known as the "flagpole library" since it was built around the city's flagpole. (Then image courtesy of the Glendale Public Library; now image, Glendale Arizona Historical Society.)

In 1938, a new library building was constructed in Murphy Park with partial funding from a Public Works Administration grant. It was Spanish in style, with brick and stucco, and painted white. In 1969, when the library had outgrown its building, it was bulldozed, and the present downtown library was erected in its place. This branch was named the Velma Teague branch after Glendale's first librarian, hired in 1935. She was the library director for most of this library's life. (Then image courtesy of the Glendale Public Library.)

FROM WATER A TOWN GREW

The library system would continue to grow with the town, creating the need for a Main Library located at 5959 West Brown Street, which opened on July 27, 1987. Located next to Sahuaro Ranch Park, the library is frequented by peacocks as well as patrons. Because of the numerous bird visits, the peacock has become somewhat of a symbol for the Glendale Public Library system. They can be found grazing on the lawn or wandering through the library's Xeriscape Gardens. (Both images courtesy of the Glendale Public Library.)

Glendale then opened its third library on July 22, 1999. This 33,500-square-foot space opened on Fifty-seventh Avenue, just north of Union Hills Road. In the vicinity of the library was, and still is, a skateboard park, a large city park, and an off-leash dog park. The Foothills Library has the distinction of being the first one in Arizona to offer a drive-up service window. The drive-up window allows library patrons to return and check items out, pick up holds, and pay fines. (Then image courtesy of the Glendale Public Library.)

In 1898, the Glendale Public Library Association was formed to help support the library, and people paid $5 a share. Edgar E. Jack bought this share on January 1, 1898. Jack was the superintendent of Rancho Del Higo. Today library service is free to Glendale residents, but nonresidents must pay $40 for one year. The fee allows the nonresident to check out materials. Nonresidents can also enjoy the variety of free programs the Glendale Public Library offers. (Then image courtesy of Glendale Arizona Historical Society; now image, the Glendale Public Library.)

In 1916, Glendale wanted to show its patriotism by erecting the tallest flagpole in Arizona. Moses Sherman, owner of the Phoenix Trolley Line, donated the 125-foot Oregon pine tree that became the 110-foot flagpole. The flagpole was 1 foot, 6 inches shorter then the *Statue of Liberty* is from crown to heel. It was replaced in 1960, when the base became rotten. Old Glory now flies from a 100-foot steel flagpole in Murphy Park. (Then image courtesy of Glendale Arizona Historical Society.)

CHAPTER

2

GLENDALE'S
FIRE AND POLICE

In 1910, with approximately 1,000 residents, Glendale elected the city's first marshal. In 1912, Glendale's fire department began. Today, with 240 firefighters and over 600 police employees, they serve and protect almost 250,000 citizens. This sculpture stands in front of fire station No. 157, located at 9658 North Fifty-ninth Avenue. It is a bas-relief brick sculpture entitled *Tribute to Firefighters*, by Jay Tchetter. Bas-relief brick is an ancient technique that is at least 3,000 years old and was first practiced in Mesopotamia.

In 1910, with approximately 1,000 residents, Glendale elected M. R. Wells to be the city's first marshal, and when necessary the city's merchants were deputized. During the 1960s, Glendale's steadily increasing population caused the police department to outgrow its home located at Glendale and Fifty-eighth Avenues. Today the Glendale Police Department is located at 6835 North Fifty-seventh Drive and has over 600 employees who serve and protect almost 250,000 citizens. (Then image courtesy of Glendale Arizona Historical Society.)

Sporting 1948 license plates, this Plymouth is one of the original police cars for the City of Glendale. It was used during a time when speeding tickets, according to old logbooks, were 50¢. In 1948, the department had two-way radios in the patrol cars and a dispatcher at the station. Today's patrol car is better-equipped and higher-tech than its predecessor. One would not find a computer in the 1948 model.

The Glendale Fire Department began in 1912, but it was not until the 1950s that the city hired its first full-time salaried fire chief. In the 1960s, the city hired its first full-time paid firefighters. Station No. 151 is considered the first and has moved after 40 years from Fifty-fifth and Orangewood Avenues to Fifty-first and Glendale Avenues. Glendale's fire department of today now has 240 firefighters, nine fire stations, and responds to approximately 40,000 calls a year.

Bought new by the city, Glendale's first fire truck was a 1917 Nash model 3017, two-ton chemical truck. Today when a person thinks about a fire truck, he or she usually thinks of red, but Glendale's trucks are painted a bright yellow called "chrome." Experts found that yellow fire trucks offer greater visibility then red ones. The Glendale Fire Department also holds the special distinction of being the first fire department to have its paramedics use Segways while working at the 2008 Super Bowl XLII. (Then image courtesy of Joy Van Wieren.)

Acquired around 1912, this fire bell once hung from the city's water tower and was used to summon the volunteer firemen, signal the town's curfew, and to alert the police at night. In 1947, the bell was moved to Murphy Park and mounted in front of the library. The bell would later take up residency outside fire station No. 151. The charming bell and its 1958 dedication plaque would follow station No. 151 when it moved to a new location in 2009. (Then image courtesy of Glendale Arizona Historical Society.)

CHAPTER 3

BEETS TO BIRDS

According to the 1913 city directory, "Glendale is located nine and one-half miles northwest of Phoenix" and "is the trade center of about 60,000 acres of the most fertile land of the Salt River Valley." At that time, Glendale was also called the "Garden City" or the "Sugar City." Before there was a railroad, produce and goods were hauled by 16 horse teams and wagons. Barely passable, the roads were full of chuckholes and were wheel-hub deep in dust. (Courtesy of the Phoenix Public Library.)

Built in 1906 to process beets into raw sugar, the sugar beet factory is located at Fifty-first and Glendale Avenues. The 52,000-square-foot factory was constructed at a cost of more than $1 million. The structure was built using bricks made on-site, when it was discovered that the soil around the factory was suited for brick making. By December 1905, two large kilns were producing 25,000 bricks per day. Unfortunately the factory never succeeded in refining beets for sugar. (Then image courtesy of Glendale Arizona Historical Society.)

By 1916, operations had stopped. Since then, different companies have leased the old factory. During the 1940s and 1950s, the Marusho Soy Sauce Company processed soy sauce. From 1938 to 1981, Squirt Soda used the factory to process soda. When Squirt stopped its operations, the TreeSweet Products Company leased the factory until 1985. In 1979, the Glendale Beet Sugar Factory was placed on the National Register of Historic Places. The old factory has remained empty since 1985 with only pigeons as tenants. (Then image courtesy of Glendale Arizona Historical Society.)

Excavated around 1908, the "Big Hole" of Glendale was located behind the factory to dump beet pulp. In 1910, cattle were run into the pit and grew fat eating the pulp. The pit was approximately 4 acres wide and 25 feet deep. When the factory closed, some thought of converting it into a lagoon, a park, and a civil defense bomb shelter. Today the huge hole is filled in, and businesses sit where cattle fed and various schemes never materialized. (Then image used with permission of *The Arizona Republic*.)

The 640-acre Rancho del Higo was founded by Samuel C. Bartlett and was hailed as proof of the success of irrigation farming in the Salt River Valley. While the ranch is gone, some of the palm trees that marked the ranch's entrance are still standing at Forty-seventh and Northern Avenues. The area is now a mix of residential and business interests. The southwestern corner was once home to a large automobile dealership but will soon be home to the city's new courthouse complex. (Then image courtesy of Glendale Arizona Historical Society.)

Manistee Ranch began as a 320-acre spread built in 1897 by Herbert W. Hamilton, a wealthy lumber baron from Wisconsin. The ranch was purchased in 1907 by Louis M. Sands, who gave it the name Manistee Ranch after his hometown in Michigan. Located along Northern Avenue, it stayed in the Sands family until being sold to the Glendale Arizona Historical Society in 1996. Today the ranch is 7 acres and is listed on the National Register of Historic Places. (Then image courtesy of Glendale Arizona Historical Society.)

In 1886, Illinois-born William Bartlett started a ranch and is believed to have named it after the saguaro cactus. Being from out of state and unfamiliar with the proper spelling, it is said that Bartlett phonetically spelled his version of the cactus "sahuaro" instead of saguaro. Sahuaro Ranch (9802 North Fifty-ninth Avenue) was one of the first ranches, making it very important to the city's history. Today's Sahuaro Ranch consists of 13 buildings, a rose garden, chickens, and peacocks. (Then image courtesy of Glendale Arizona Historical Society.)

On "Chicken Day," May 20, 1921, Glendale donated 10 acres at Fifty-ninth and Maryland Avenues to establish the U.S. Experimental Poultry Station. The farm's poultry included chickens, turkeys, and a dozen ostriches. In 1968, Harry Bonsall Sr. and Sen. Carl Hayden held negotiations with the government, who in turn deeded the land back to the city. It became a city park, known as "Chicken Park." In 1982, the name was changed to its current name—Bonsall Park. (Then image courtesy of National Archives and Records Administration.)

Cowboys once herded ostriches on this field near Ninety-ninth and Glendale Avenues. The City of Glendale provides this trivia, "Ostrich feathers were a huge business in Glendale from the late 1800s until around 1914 when World War I began. It was said that their diet of Glendale-grown alfalfa provided the feathers with a unique luster not found anywhere else in the world." In 1910, a total of 4,023 ostriches were plucked for a value of $1,365,000. Feathers sold for around $75 per pound. (Then image courtesy of Glendale Arizona Historical Society.)

Until 1914 and World War 1, small farms found ostriches more profitable than cattle, since an ostrich cost less to feed and had a crop of feathers every eight months until it was 50 or 60 years old. The Victorian woman pictured is wearing an ostrich plume hat. Styles changed over the years, and today plumes are often seen on costumes, boas, and even on the harnesses of carriage horses, as seen here. (Then image courtesy of the Graphics Fairy.)

CHAPTER 4

BUNGALOWS, BUILDINGS, AND BUSINESSES

For Glendale's first decade, irrigation farming was the main occupation. The establishment of the Glendale Ice Company in 1910 made the city the largest produce shipping point in Arizona by 1920. It also provided the first power plant, which the city bought around 1914 to provide power to residential and commercial customers. Smaller business ventures soon attracted new people to Glendale, with World War II bringing thousands. The ice plant located at Glendale and Fifty-ninth Avenues was demolished in 1990. (Courtesy of Glendale Arizona Historical Society.)

Looking east down Glendale Avenue in the 1930s, one can see Murphy Park to the left. Murphy Park is not big, only 3 acres, with an amphitheater for events, but it is the heart of downtown Glendale. The park is named for W. J. Murphy, the city founder, who donated the land in 1909. Murphy Park is a center of activity with a variety of festivals and events. The park was once home to the tallest flagpole in the state. (Then image courtesy of Glendale Arizona Historical Society.)

In 1912, banker C. H. Tinker moved to Glendale. Four years later, he organized the Security State Bank. Two years after that, he moved and renamed the bank as the First National Bank of Glendale. Since 1918, the bank has remained the only unchanged commercial building left downtown. It is also Glendale's only example of the Beaux-Arts style and has changed very little. Located at 6838 North Fifty-eighth Drive, the building is now the law office of Richard Coffinger. (Then image courtesy of Glendale Arizona Historical Society.)

Pratt's Pets and Feed is one of Glendale's oldest businesses. Originally called Pratt's Feed and Supply, the store's first customers were farmers. Later their customer base consisted of the horse riders, and today it is the pet lovers. Pratt's was built in 1953 on Glendale and Fifty-second Avenues (5237 West Glendale Avenue). A third-generation Pratt owns and operates the small family store with its menagerie of exotic birds, puppies, kittens, farm animals, and reptiles, as well as pet supplies and feed. (Then image courtesy of the Pratt family.)

Emerson Wilcken Pratt (1901–2001) originally started the Pratt's feed business. Born in Chihuahua, Mexico, his family was forced to leave Mexico by the infamous Pancho Villa and moved to Arizona. Emerson worked for the Farmers Cooperative and was given the opportunity to purchase the business, which he did, and Pratt's Feed and Supply was born. Pratt's Pets and Feed still operates a mill to mix different feeds, mostly bird mixes. The mill is located next to the store. (Then image courtesy of the Pratt family.)

In 1911, Van and Tuck Sine opened a hardware store on Fifty-eighth Drive in downtown Glendale. The livery stable was torn down to build the store. Pictured here in 1949, there was a boardinghouse above the store. Several years ago, the City of Glendale bought and restored the Sines' original building to what it almost looked like in 1918. Now seven city departments work out of what employees call the "Sine Building." (Then image courtesy of Glendale Arizona Historical Society.)

BUNGALOWS, BUILDINGS, AND BUSINESSES

A new front was added to the Sine Hardware building in 1951. In the 1960s, Sine remodeled the store but constructed a new one in 1991 at 7150 North Fifty-first Avenue. It is now Sine Ace Hardware. The Sine family was enterprising and owned several businesses: Sine Brothers and Sons welding company, Sine Garage, and Sine Brothers Company machine shop. The city's water supply tower was owned by Holmes Sine, who sold it to the City of Glendale in 1915. (Then image courtesy of Glendale Arizona Historical Society.)

Robert W. Cole purchased three lots and built his two-story general store at 7005 North Fifty-eighth Avenue in 1919. It was the first business on this block. In the 1940s, it was Sprouse-Reitz 5 & 10¢ Store. Later the store became Larry Glazman's Boot Barn and Egglestons apparel store. In 1997, Jim Eggleston passed the store to daughter Kathy Munninger, who changed the name. Kathy's Korner Boot Barn survived into the 1990s, but is now the Tea Shoppe. (Then image courtesy of Glendale Arizona Historical Society.)

BUNGALOWS, BUILDINGS, AND BUSINESSES

Downtown Glendale was vibrant from the 1940s to 1960s. Citizens went to see movies, shop at the stores, buy groceries, and meet at the drugstore's soda fountains. The south side of Glendale Avenue in 1960 was home to Coury's Market, Miller Shoes, and Ryan-Evans Drug Store. Then, in the 1960s, the retail industry followed the more mobile (thanks to the automobile) population. To save the ailing downtown, the city council formed the Downtown Development Advisory Board. Today the shops are antique stores. (Then image courtesy of Glendale Community College.)

Downtown stores were booming in the 1960s, and the area was the center of activity for everyone. Glendale and Fifty-eighth Avenues were home to Leonard's, HFC Loans, and Glendale Office Supply. Then, in 1973, Valley West Mall opened with all its stores under one air-conditioned roof, and downtown began to ail as stores closed. During the 1990s, the merchants organized to promote downtown. Instead of businesses leaving, stores were opening, and today there are antique and specialty shops in historic downtown. (Then image courtesy of Glendale Community College.)

BUNGALOWS, BUILDINGS, AND BUSINESSES

Glendale Woman's Club started in 1901 as a "Self Culture Club." By 1907, the group needed its own clubhouse. The first private donation of $5 was given by a member using her state fair prize money for the best cake baked with sugar from the town's beet factory. By 1912, enough money was raised to build one of the first Woman's Club clubhouses in Arizona. Located at 7032 North Fifty-sixth Avenue, it remains active and at that location today. (Then image courtesy of Glendale Arizona Historical Society.)

Through the years, members of the Sands family have made significant contributions to Glendale. Sands Chevrolet, which opened in Glendale in 1934, was one of them. Louis Sands started several businesses, including the Sands Motor Company—the first car dealership in Glendale. It later changed its name to Sands Chevrolet. It is still Sands Chevrolet today and in the same location. The Sands staff isn't sure what was here first, the railroad tracks or the Sands dealership. (Then image courtesy of Louis "Buzz" Sands IV of Sands Chevrolet.)

BUNGALOWS, BUILDINGS, AND BUSINESSES

Metro Music Center opened in 1960 and closed in 2009. Located at 4734 West Glendale Avenue, customers could find the store by looking for its bright yellow music note–shaped sign. According to the store's owner, Tracy Williams, generations of Glendale schoolchildren, band teachers, and other musicians—including Alice Cooper, Three Dog Night, and other valley bands that became famous—once shopped at Metro Music. The City of Glendale is attempting to rejuvenate Glendale Avenue by attracting developers.

Listed on the National Register of Historic Places, this 1922 craftsman bungalow resides at Fifty-eighth and Myrtle Avenues in Catlin Court. Until recently, it was the Marty Robbins Museum. Born in Glendale in 1925, Robbins was known to sleep at the house. Bungalows were homes from the arts and crafts era (1800s–1900s). Homebuyers purchased their houses through Sears catalogs, and their kit would arrive by train. This is also why bungalow homes are often found close to rail lines. (Then image courtesy of Lauren Russell, the Arts and Crafts Society.)

MODERN HOME No. 264P237

When comparing prices, consider that all our houses have **double floors** on first floor, and are enclosed with **good matched sheathing.**

First story inside floors, trim, doors, etc., furnished in clear red oak for $121.00 extra.

This Speaks Well for Quality.

404 N. Olive St., Media, Penn.

Sears, Roebuck and Co., Chicago, Ill.

Gentlemen:—I received your lumber and after a thorough examination must say that the quality is the best I ever purchased. You may use my name if you wish as I will gladly recommend you to anyone calling on me by letter or person.

Yours very truly,
EDMOND E. DICKENSON,
Contractor and Builder.

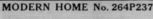

Plan.

$1,204.00

For $1,204.00 we will furnish all the material to build this Fi Room Bungalow, consisting of Mill Work, Medicine Cabinet, Le ber, Lath, Shingles, Flooring, Finishing Lumber, Building Pap Pipe, Gutter, Sash Weights, Hardware and Painting Material. EXTRAS, as we guarantee enough material at the above price build this bungalow according to our plans.

By allowing a fair price for labor, cement, brick and plas which we do not furnish, this bungalow can be built for ab $2,542.00, including all material and labor.

For Our Offer of Free Plans See Page 6.

IN BUNGALOW No. 264P237 we have one of those practical designs so much in favor the Pacific Coast. Built in the proper surroundings and given the proper color treat a bungalow of this kind will be an ornament to any community and a constant sour pleasure to the owner. A good color scheme would be green for the body of the which is sided with shingles, with white trim and green for the roof.

The floor plan of this bungalow covers a space of about 29 feet by 47 feet, allowing f floor space than is provided in the ordinary bungalow. The big living room, well lighted d room and sleeping porch in the rear have been given special treatment. Note the big n in the living room with windows on each side and the swinging windows in the dining r Bungalows of this design and construction sell readily for $3,500.00 to $4,000.00; material which we furnish for only $1,204.00 is guaranteed to be first class in every res There is absolutely nothing cheap about it but the price.

First Floor.

From the large front porch a handsome Craftsman door leads directly into the living room which is 25 feet by 14 feet. To the right is a large rustic brick mantel with a window on each side of it. In the opposite corner of the living room is a clothes closet. In the opening between the living room and dining room are paneled pedestals with Craftsman brackets in the corners of the cased opening above, which add a great deal to the effect and thoroughly conform with the architectural appearance of the beamed ceiling in the dining room. The dining room is 14 feet 10 inches by 11 feet 6 inches with a door leading to the small center hall and one leading to the kitchen. In the right wall of the dining room is a group of four casement sash opening on hinges. The kitchen is provided with two closets to take the place of a pantry. There is a broom closet in one corner and a cooler in the other. One door leading to the center hall, one leading direct to the basement and one to the outside porch. From the center hall one can enter into the two bedrooms, bathroom, dining room, kitchen or open air sleeping porch. The bathroom is of fair size and provided with a linen closet. The house is finished with clear Crafts man yellow pine trim throughout with the exception of the front door which is oak and the kitchen door which is white pine.

Basement.

Excavated basement under rear half of the house is 7 feet high with a cement floor.

Height of Ceilings.

Basement, 7 feet high from floor to joists. Rooms on the main floor are 9 feet high.

This bungalow is built on a concrete foundation: No. 1 yellow pine fr construction. Sided and roofed with red cedar shingles.

Can be built on a lot 40 feet wide.

Complete Warm Air Heating Plant, for soft coal, extra $69
Complete Warm Air Heating Plant, for hard coal, extra 71

If estimates and specifications for plumbing and hot water or ste heating systems are desired write for them, mentioning Modern Home 264P237 in your request.

SEARS, ROEBUCK AND CO.

CHICAGO, ILLINOIS.

The Spicery, or Messinger, house is located at 7141 North Fifty-ninth Avenue and is Glendale's oldest house. The home's first owner was Victor E. Messinger, who was Glendale's first town clerk and librarian. Messinger built the house in 1895. He lived here until 1936, when it was purchased by the Brewster family. They owned the home until 1988, when it became the Spicery Tea Room Restaurant. Built in the Queen Anne Victorian style, it now sits empty. (Then image courtesy of City of Glendale.)

The Gillett Building is the oldest downtown structure. Located at 5825 West Glendale Avenue, it was home to Glendale's first bank. Charles L. Gillett constructed and opened the Glendale State Bank in 1909. For protection from burglars, Gillett kept his pet wildcat in the basement. In addition to the bank, the building was home to Wood's Pharmacy and the Glendale Taxi Company. The upstairs had meeting space. Today the current owner is doing restoration on the structure. (Then image courtesy of Glendale Arizona Historical Society.)

BUNGALOWS, BUILDINGS, AND BUSINESSES

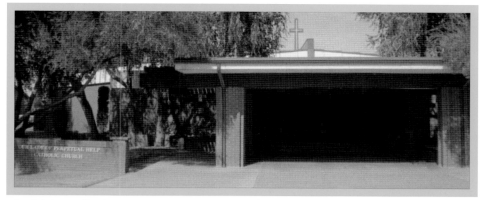

Glendale's small adobe Catholic church was destroyed by fire in 1937. When the congregation rebuilt the church, they used black rocks, giving the church the nickname the "Rock Church." Given the official name Our Lady of Perpetual Help, the church acquired acreage in 1953 on which a school was built. More buildings were added over the next 20 years, including a new sanctuary to replace the old Rock Church. Our Lady of Perpetual Help is located at 5614 West Orangewood Avenue. (Then image courtesy of Glendale Arizona Historical Society.)

The Christian Church organized in Glendale in 1914 and in 1917 built this church. The structure is an unusual and large example of the craftsman-style bungalow. It is the only bungalow church in Arizona. The church was designed and built by C. B. Woodruff, a Wilcox, Arizona, architect. Located at 7154 North Fifty-eighth Drive, the church still stands and is currently occupied by Manor at Catlin Court, an all-occasion reception center that can accommodate up to 250 guests. (Then image courtesy of Glendale Arizona Historical Society.)

BUNGALOWS, BUILDINGS, AND BUSINESSES

In 1894, Methodists did not have a church of their own, but that would change when the 1897 Methodist Episcopal Church was built. The church was used until 1920, when the sanctuary was sold and moved. The new church was not completed until 1928 and is still used today. The church was designed as a grand two-story Gothic structure with a three-story buttressed corner tower. First United Methodist Church of Glendale is located at 7102 North Fifty-eighth Drive. (Then image courtesy of Glendale Arizona Historical Society.)

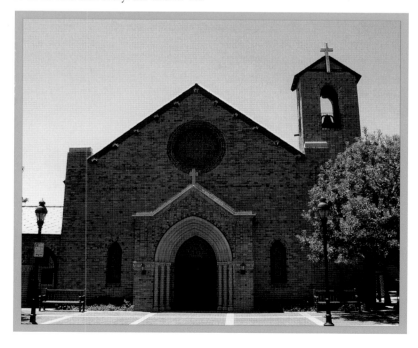

To make room for the new church in 1920, the parsonage was moved to another part of the property. Now known as the First United Methodist Church, the congregation, needing to expand again, moved the parsonage north to Second (known as Fifty-Eighth Avenue today) and Palmaire Avenues, retaining ownership until 1949. Today the old parsonage is a gift boutique in the Catlin Court Historic District. This older home is also the second-oldest home in historic Catlin Court. (Then image courtesy of Glendale Arizona Historical Society.)

BUNGALOWS, BUILDINGS, AND BUSINESSES

In the 1920s, Grace Evangelical Lutheran Church's services were held at various locations throughout Glendale. Arrangements were made to purchase land at Fifty-sixth and Palmaire Avenues, and by May 1927 services were held in the new chapel. Then, in 1952, another church was built, and it would be the congregation's house of worship until 2005, when the current church and fellowship hall were dedicated. The old chapels still remain on the property as a conference room, church/school office, and kindergarten room. (Then image courtesy of Grace Lutheran Church.)

The name Molokan is derived from the Russian word for milk drinkers, because Molokans refused to follow the tradition of not consuming dairy products during Lent. The first 35 Molokan families arrived in Glendale in 1911 to discover that the land purchased for them was still covered by cactus and overrun with snakes and scorpions. This Russian Molokan church is located at 7402 Griffin Avenue, replacing the first one from the 1950s, and it is still standing today mostly unchanged. (Then image courtesy of Marshall E. Bowen.)

Bungalows, Buildings, and Businesses

In 1960, Glendale's first hospital, Northwest, was located on Northern and Sixty-first Avenues. It served Glendale's population of less than 34,000. It would later be renamed Samaritan Hospital. In 1983, the hospital was moved to a larger location on Fifty-fifth Avenue and Thunderbird Road and was renamed again, this time to Thunderbird Banner Medical Center. The Salvation Army Glendale Corps Community Center now resides in the old Northwest Hospital building. (Then image courtesy of Glendale Arizona Historical Society.)

Banner Thunderbird has had a presence in Glendale since 1960. As the population grew so did the need for a larger facility. The hospital moved to Fifty-fifth Avenue and Thunderbird Road in 1983 and continues to grow in beds and buildings. The new patient tower will be the tallest structure in the Northwest Valley. Once expansion is completed, Banner Thunderbird will offer 582 private rooms and will be the largest hospital in the Northwest Valley. (Both images courtesy of Banner Thunderbird Medical Center.)

Festivals, such as this 1932 Fiesta Patria, are part of Glendale's history. The city still celebrates throughout the year with a variety of events. It is all about the lights at Glendale Glitters and Glows, and it is a chocolate lover's paradise at the Chocolate Affair. Vendors and crafters—such as hometown favorite the Cerreta Candy Company—showcase their talents and wares. Cerreta's, located at 5345 West Glendale Avenue, has been making chocolate in Glendale for over 30 years. (Then image courtesy of Glendale Arizona Historical Society.)

Cabela's, the "World's Foremost Outfitter," opened its 15th destination retail store in Glendale in July 2006. The 160,000-square-foot store is located at 9380 West Glendale Avenue. There aren't many stores that are also tourist destinations. The store features museum-quality taxidermy animals featured in recreations of their habitats and huge aquariums. An upstairs cafeteria features buffalo burgers, venison bratwurst, and elk sandwiches. It takes about 300 employees to operate the Glendale Cabela's. (Then image courtesy of Cabela's.)

In 1957, Salt River Project's (SRP) Agua Fria Generating Station, located at 7302 West Northern Avenue, began operating. By 1984, the plant would generate nearly 600,000 kilowatts. Today the plant contains a 200-kilowatt solar-generating unit, three steam-generating units, and three combustion turbine generators. In the valley since 1903, SRP is the nation's third-largest public power utility. In 1904, SRP was recognized by the U.S. Department of the Interior as the first reclamation project of the 1902 Reclamation Act. (Then image courtesy of Glendale Arizona Historical Society.)

Built in the 1970s, Valley West was a fully enclosed shopping mall located near Fifty-seventh and Northern Avenues. In the 1990s, the mall changed its name to Manistee Town Center, but it still closed. Prior to demolition, it was leased out to Hollywood for the 2002 film *Eight Legged Freaks*. The mall scenes were shot in the abandoned center. In March 2004, Northern Crossing Power Center opened and is a successfully redeveloped center with Lowe's and WalMart as anchors. (Then image courtesy of Glendale Arizona Historical Society.)

BUNGALOWS, BUILDINGS, AND BUSINESSES

CHAPTER 5

UNCLE SAM COMES TO GLENDALE TO TRAIN AND STAYS

World War II brought Thunderbird and Luke Fields. Thunderbird, to train civilian pilots for the army, began as a joint project of Hollywood producer Leland Hayward, Air Service pilot John H. Connelly, and *Life* magazine photographer John Swope. Luke Field followed after Arizona was chosen for an Army Air Corps training field. Thunderbird Field is now Thunderbird School of Global Management, and Luke is now Luke Air Force Base and home to the world's greatest F-16 fighter pilots. (Photograph by John Swope, courtesy of John Swope Trust.)

In 1941, producer Leland Hayward and Jimmy Stewart teamed with other stars, such as Henry Fonda and Cary Grant, to invest in Thunderbird Field, a flying school located at 15249 North Fifty-ninth Avenue. Well-known artist Millard Sheets designed the layout of the airbase so that from the air it would resemble the mythical Anasazi god of thunder called the Thunderbird. The Thunderbird shape is not as obvious today, as neighborhoods and businesses have filled in around what is now a business school. (Then image courtesy of Thunderbird Archives.)

UNCLE SAME COMES TO GLENDALE TO TRAIN AND STAYS

Named one of the army's most efficient training bases, Thunderbird Army Air Field was also known as the "Country Club of the Air Corps." During World War II, the hangars on the airfield housed the popular yellow, bi-wing Stearman trainers. These PT Stearmans were also known as "Thunderbirds." They were often seen flying over Glendale. After Thunderbird Field became the American Institute for Foreign Trade, the hangar became a parking garage and later an activity center. (Then image by John Swope, courtesy of John Swope Trust.)

The Tower, built in late 1939, served as the air-control tower and officers' quarters for Thunderbird Army Air Field. When the airfield became a school in 1946, the Tower remained and has housed faculty offices, a student lounge, the Tower Café, and the school newspaper. The Tower has been the icon of the school for 60 years, but in January 2006 it closed and was made off-limits due to structural issues. Efforts are underway to restore it. (Then image by John Swope, courtesy of John Swope Trust.)

UNCLE SAME COMES TO GLENDALE TO TRAIN AND STAYS

Thunderbird Field was also the start of the aerobatic squadron the Flying Thunderbirds. On June 1, 1953, the Flying Thunderbirds Squadron was activated after only 6 months of training. They had unofficial status as the 3600th Air Demonstration Team at Luke AFB. Their debut exhibition was a week later at Luke. The squadron moved in June 1956 to their current headquarters at Nellis Air Force Base in Nevada. Pictured from 1955 are the F-84F Thunderstreaks, and from 2008 are the Thunderbird F-16s. (Both images courtesy of U.S. Air Force public domain.)

The American Institute for Foreign Trade opened its doors on October 1, 1946, just six months after its founders purchased the deactivated Army Air Forces Training Base. The school is now known as the Thunderbird School of Global Management. It has been ranked by *U.S. News and World Report* magazine as the number one school for international business in the United States. Thunderbird is the first and oldest graduate management school focused exclusively on global business. (Then image courtesy of the Thunderbird Archives.)

A representative sent to Arizona in the 1940s chose a site for a U.S. Army Air Corps training field, and construction started on Litchfield Park Air Base on March 29, 1941. When the Luke base in Pearl Harbor was transferred to the navy in June 1941, they released the name to the new Arizona base. The base was renamed Luke Field after Phoenix-born (1897) Medal of Honor recipient Lt. Frank Luke Jr. Pictured are the main gates in 1995 and 2009. (Both images courtesy of Glendale Arizona Historical Society.)

During World War II, Luke was the largest fighter-training base in the Air Corps, graduating more than 12,000 pilots by February 1944. Unfortunately by 1946 the number of pilots trained dropped to 299, and the base was deactivated on November 30, 1946. Then came the Korean Conflict, and Luke field was reactivated on February 1, 1951, as Luke Air Force Base. Today the Luke base trains F1 pilots. Pictured is a Lockheed F-104G from the past and today's F-16 jets. (Both images courtesy of U.S. Air Force public domain.)

UNCLE SAME COMES TO GLENDALE TO TRAIN AND STAYS

CHAPTER 6

FROM A ONE-ROOM SCHOOLHOUSE TO UNIVERSITIES

In 1895, Glendale built its first school, a grammar school. In 1911, the town dedicated its first high school with much spectacle. The city fathers constructed a high school despite the fact that attending high school was not required in a thriving agricultural community. Today there are several elementary and high schools, the American Graduate School of International Management, Midwestern University, Glendale Community College, and Arizona State University's West Campus. Pictured is all that is left of the original classrooms. (Courtesy of Glendale Arizona Historical Society.)

With the influx of people after the century's first decade, Glendale's elementary school enrollment soared to 260 by 1912, making the 1895 brick schoolhouse inadequate. Taking steps towards better education, in 1913 the citizens approved bonds, and the Glendale Grammar School was built. An auditorium with seating for more than 1,000 became the focal point of the school. The auditorium survives today. The present school is known as Landmark Elementary School and is located at 5730 West Myrtle Avenue. (Then image courtesy of Glendale Arizona Historical Society.)

In 1895, Glendale's first school was built. The Glendale Grammar School was a four-room schoolhouse constructed with locally made brick. Fearful of tuberculosis, the school was built on an experimental plan called the "unit system." By 1913, there would be 36 separate classrooms. This design also minimized the risk of fire hazards. The only other reminder of the "unit" classrooms is Room 35, which sits among the newer classrooms. The classroom is also on the National Register of Historic Places. (Then image courtesy of Glendale Arizona Historical Society.)

Glendale opened its first high school in 1911 inside a storeroom with 20 students. Enrollment increased to 58 students and the faculty to three. Despite the fact that attending high school was not required in a thriving agricultural community, there was a public demand for a high school, and in 1912 the Glendale High School was constructed. U.S. vice president Thomas R. Marshall (pictured above) delivered one of the dedication speeches for the new high school. (Then image courtesy of Glendale Arizona Historical Society.)

FROM A ONE-ROOM SCHOOLHOUSE TO UNIVERSITIES

The school was dedicated on February 12, 1913, welcoming 101 students and a six-member faculty. The original auditorium still stands on the campus, and legend has it that the building is haunted by an active ghost named Joe. It is the oldest high school in Arizona that still stands at its original location. Glendale High School boasts former pitcher for the Chicago White Sox Lerrin LaGrow as a notable graduate. (Then image courtesy of Glendale High School.)

Glendale Community College (GCC) opened its doors in 1965 and is a part of the Maricopa County Community College District, which is the largest community college district in the United States. The 147-acre campus is located at Fifty-ninth and Olive Avenues. The first day that class was held at the college's current location was September 16, 1966. The school enrolls about 30,000 students per year and offers 1,000-plus courses. Notable students of GCC include shock-rocker Alice Cooper. (Then image courtesy of Glendale Community College.)

FROM A ONE-ROOM SCHOOLHOUSE TO UNIVERSITIES

Construction began on Arizona State University, West Campus, in 1986. The first completed building was the Fletcher Library in 1989. The remaining structures were complete in 1991. The three-story library also houses Technopolis (a computing center) and the Learning Enhancement Center (a tutoring center). Originally ASU West was designed to offer only junior- and senior-level courses, but in 2001 it expanded the campus to offer a lower-division curriculum. ASU West had its first freshman class on August 20, 2001. (Then image courtesy of Arizona State University, West Campus.)

Midwestern University is a nonprofit, private graduate school of medicine. The university started as one college, over a century ago, training physicians only. Today it has two campuses that train health professionals in many different fields. Midwestern University's Glendale campus was founded in 1995. The campus sits on 135 acres with buildings that are used as academic classrooms, state-of-the-art laboratories, student housing, and an on-campus osteopathic clinic. The university is located on Fifty-ninth Avenue near Utopia Road. (Then image courtesy of Midwestern University.)

CHAPTER 7

GLENDALE'S GOT GAME

Where cotton grew and cattle pastured, football and hockey are now played. Glendale has become a sports and entertainment mecca. It hosts events such as the Super Bowl, Rolling Stones and Elton John concerts, trade shows, and Wrestlemania. In 2006, the City of Glendale developed the advertising campaign "Glendale's Got Game" to promote and highlight Glendale's sports and entertainment as the city prepared for Super Bowl XLIII. Today's Glendale has facilities for football, ice hockey, and baseball spring training.

The land at the intersection of Arizona State Route 101—or "Loop 101"—and Glendale Avenue is Westgate City Center. It is a 223-acre development comprised of sports and entertainment complexes such as the stadium, arena, and a 320-room Renaissance Hotel and Conference Center. Before this $1 billion development, the area looked very different in the 1950s. It was cotton fields and pastures for sheep and cattle. Some of the land around the complex is still used for cotton and sheep until they are sold. (Then image courtesy of the Tolmachoff family.)

Jobing.com Arena is home to the National Hockey League's Phoenix Coyotes. The arena, located at 9400 West Maryland Avenue and finished on December 26, 2003, is owned by the City of Glendale and until 2008 was known as Glendale Arena. It is also an entertainment venue and was named Pollstar Best New Concert Venue of the Year Award in 2004. The arena has hosted some of the biggest names in entertainment, such as Stevie Wonder, Hannah Montana (Miley Cyrus), the Rolling Stones, and Elton John. (Then image courtesy of Jobing.com Arena.)

Where cattle and sheep once grazed is now home to the University of Phoenix Stadium. The stadium, residing at 1 Cardinals Drive, opened on August 1, 2006. Home of the National Football League's Arizona Cardinals, it is the first stadium in North America capable of completely moving its grass playing field in and out of the stadium, and it is considered an architectural icon. Where cotton and alfalfa once grew, Super Bowl XLII was held. (Then image courtesy of Global Spectrum.)

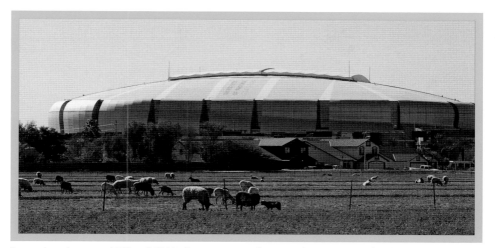

Somewhere between 1905 and 1910, this custom-built plow is pictured preparing the land for crops. Now, where alfalfa fields once grew, the University of Phoenix Stadium rises up like the huge barrel cactus it is loosely modeled after. The stadium is also the venue for concerts and trade shows and hosted Wrestlemania XXVI in 2010. Sheep still graze in fields near the stadium, a reminder of Glendale's agricultural past. (Then image courtesy of Glendale Arizona Historical Society.)

www.arcadiapublishing.com

Discover books about the town where you grew up, the cities where your friends and families live, the town where your parents met, or even that retirement spot you've been dreaming about. Our Web site provides history lovers with exclusive deals, advanced notification about new titles, e-mail alerts of author events, and much more.

MADE IN THE USA

Arcadia Publishing, the leading local history publisher in the United States, is committed to making history accessible and meaningful through publishing books that celebrate and preserve the heritage of America's people and places. Consistent with our mission to preserve history on a local level, this book was printed in South Carolina on American-made paper and manufactured entirely in the United States.

This book carries the accredited Forest Stewardship Council (FSC) label and is printed on 100 percent FSC-certified paper. Products carrying the FSC label are independently certified to assure consumers that they come from forests that are managed to meet the social, economic, and ecological needs of present and future generations.

FSC
Mixed Sources
Product group from well-managed forests and other controlled sources

Cert no. SW-COC-001530
www.fsc.org
© 1996 Forest Stewardship Council

Find Your Place in History.